55 Sandwiches Recipes for Home

By: Kelly Johnson

Table of Contents

- Classic BLT Sandwich
- Turkey Club Sandwich
- Grilled Chicken Caesar Wrap
- Caprese Panini
- Reuben Sandwich
- Cubano (Cuban Sandwich)
- Veggie Hummus Wrap
- Philly Cheesesteak Sandwich
- Tuna Melt
- Egg Salad Sandwich
- Pesto Chicken Panini
- Mediterranean Veggie Sandwich
- Spicy Chicken Avocado Wrap
- French Dip Sandwich
- BBQ Pulled Pork Sandwich
- Smoked Salmon Bagel Sandwich
- Roast Beef and Horseradish Wrap
- Chickpea Salad Sandwich (Vegan)
- Italian Submarine Sandwich
- Chicken Shawarma Wrap
- California Turkey Club Wrap
- Grilled Cheese with Tomato Soup
- Turkey Cranberry Panini
- Shrimp Po' Boy Sandwich
- Buffalo Chicken Wrap
- Avocado and Bacon Grilled Cheese
- Chicken Pesto Ciabatta
- Classic Peanut Butter and Jelly
- Gyro Sandwich with Tzatziki Sauce
- Smashed Chickpea Avocado Sandwich (Vegan)
- Monte Cristo Sandwich
- Turkey Apple Cheddar Panini
- Banh Mi Sandwich
- Portobello Mushroom Burger (Vegetarian)
- Spicy Italian Sausage Sub

- Chicken Caesar Salad Wrap
- Croque Monsieur
- Crab Cake Sandwich
- Hawaiian BBQ Chicken Sandwich
- The Elvis Sandwich (Peanut Butter, Banana, and Bacon)
- Chipotle Turkey Panini
- Chicken and Waffle Sandwich
- Mediterranean Chicken Pita
- Caprese Grilled Cheese
- Smoked Turkey and Cranberry Wrap
- Spicy Tofu Banh Mi (Vegan)
- Southwestern Black Bean Burger (Vegetarian)
- Grilled Eggplant and Mozzarella Panini
- BBQ Jackfruit Sandwich (Vegan)
- Turkey Reuben Wrap
- Portobello Mushroom and Goat Cheese Panini (Vegetarian)
- California Veggie Wrap
- Pastrami on Rye
- Moroccan Lamb Pita
- Turkey Avocado Ranch Wrap

Classic BLT Sandwich

Ingredients:

- 8 slices of thick-cut bacon
- 4 lettuce leaves (Romaine or iceberg)
- 2 large tomatoes, thinly sliced
- 8 slices of your favorite bread
- Mayonnaise
- Salt and pepper to taste

Instructions:

Cook the bacon in a skillet over medium heat until crispy. Drain excess fat on a paper towel.
Toast the slices of bread to your liking.
Spread a generous layer of mayonnaise on one side of each slice of bread.
On one slice, layer lettuce leaves, followed by tomato slices. Season the tomatoes with a pinch of salt and pepper.
Place the crispy bacon on top of the tomatoes.
Top with another slice of bread, mayo side down, to create the sandwich.
Repeat the process for the remaining sandwiches.
Cut each sandwich in half diagonally and serve immediately.

Enjoy the classic combination of crispy bacon, fresh lettuce, and juicy tomatoes in this timeless BLT sandwich!

Turkey Club Sandwich

Ingredients:

- 8 slices of turkey breast
- 8 slices of bacon, cooked until crispy
- 6 slices of your favorite bread
- 4 lettuce leaves
- 2 tomatoes, thinly sliced
- Mayonnaise
- Mustard
- Salt and pepper to taste

Instructions:

Toast the slices of bread to your liking.
Spread a layer of mayonnaise on one side of each slice of bread.
On one slice, place two lettuce leaves, followed by 4 slices of turkey.
Add a second slice of bread on top, mayo side down.
Spread a layer of mustard on the top of the second slice of bread.
Add 4 slices of crispy bacon on top of the mustard.
Add a third slice of bread, mayo side down.
Place tomato slices on top of the third slice of bread and season with salt and pepper.
Add the final slice of bread, mayo side up, to complete the sandwich.
Repeat the process for the remaining sandwiches.
Secure each sandwich with toothpicks and cut in half before serving.

Enjoy this classic Turkey Club Sandwich with layers of turkey, bacon, lettuce, and tomato for a satisfying and flavorful meal!

Grilled Chicken Caesar Wrap

Ingredients:

For Grilled Chicken:

- 2 boneless, skinless chicken breasts
- 2 tablespoons olive oil
- 1 teaspoon garlic powder
- Salt and black pepper to taste

For Caesar Dressing:

- 1/2 cup mayonnaise
- 2 tablespoons grated Parmesan cheese
- 1 tablespoon Dijon mustard
- 1 clove garlic, minced
- 1 tablespoon lemon juice
- Salt and black pepper to taste

For Wrap Assembly:

- 4 large tortillas or wraps
- Romaine lettuce leaves, washed and dried
- 1 cup cherry tomatoes, halved
- 1/2 cup grated Parmesan cheese
- Croutons (optional)

Instructions:

Preheat the grill or grill pan over medium-high heat.
In a bowl, mix olive oil, garlic powder, salt, and pepper. Coat the chicken breasts with this mixture.
Grill the chicken breasts for 6-8 minutes per side or until fully cooked. Allow them to rest for a few minutes before slicing into strips.
In a small bowl, whisk together mayonnaise, grated Parmesan, Dijon mustard, minced garlic, lemon juice, salt, and pepper to create the Caesar dressing.
Lay out the tortillas, and spread a generous amount of Caesar dressing over each one.
Place a layer of Romaine lettuce leaves on each tortilla.

Add sliced grilled chicken on top of the lettuce.
Sprinkle halved cherry tomatoes and grated Parmesan cheese over the chicken.
Optionally, add croutons for an extra crunch.
Fold in the sides of each tortilla and roll tightly to form a wrap.
Secure with toothpicks if needed and cut in half before serving.

Enjoy this Grilled Chicken Caesar Wrap, a delightful combination of grilled chicken, crisp veggies, and flavorful Caesar dressing!

Caprese Panini

Ingredients:

- 8 slices of ciabatta bread
- 2 large tomatoes, thinly sliced
- 1 ball of fresh mozzarella, thinly sliced
- Fresh basil leaves
- Balsamic glaze
- Olive oil
- Salt and black pepper to taste

Instructions:

Preheat a panini press or grill pan.
Brush one side of each slice of ciabatta bread with olive oil.
On the unoiled side of half the slices, layer tomato slices, mozzarella slices, and fresh basil leaves.
Drizzle balsamic glaze over the ingredients and season with salt and black pepper.
Top with the remaining slices of ciabatta bread, oiled side facing out.
Place the sandwiches on the preheated panini press or grill pan.
Grill for 3-5 minutes, or until the bread is toasted and the cheese is melted.
Carefully remove the sandwiches from the press or pan, and let them rest for a minute.
Cut the paninis in half diagonally and serve immediately.

Enjoy this classic Caprese Panini, featuring the timeless combination of tomatoes, mozzarella, and fresh basil!

Reuben Sandwich

Ingredients:

- 8 slices of rye bread
- 1 pound thinly sliced corned beef
- 1 cup sauerkraut, drained
- 8 slices Swiss cheese
- 1/2 cup Thousand Island dressing
- Butter for spreading
- Pickles (optional, for serving)

Instructions:

Preheat a griddle or skillet over medium heat.
Butter one side of each slice of rye bread.
On the unbuttered side of half the slices, layer corned beef, sauerkraut, and Swiss cheese.
Spread Thousand Island dressing on the unbuttered side of the remaining slices of bread.
Place the dressing-covered slices on top of the layered slices to form sandwiches, buttered side facing out.
Grill the sandwiches on the preheated griddle or skillet for 3-4 minutes per side, or until the bread is toasted, and the cheese is melted.
Remove from heat and let them rest for a minute.
Optionally, cut the sandwiches in half diagonally before serving.
Serve with pickles on the side if desired.

Enjoy this classic Reuben Sandwich, a delicious combination of corned beef, sauerkraut, Swiss cheese, and Thousand Island dressing!

Cubano (Cuban Sandwich)

Ingredients:

- 4 Cuban bread rolls or sub rolls
- 1 pound roast pork, thinly sliced
- 1/2 pound ham, thinly sliced
- 8 slices Swiss cheese
- 1 cup dill pickles, thinly sliced
- Mustard, to taste
- Butter for spreading

Instructions:

Preheat a griddle or panini press.
Slice the Cuban bread rolls in half lengthwise.
On the bottom half of each roll, layer roast pork, ham, Swiss cheese, and sliced pickles.
Spread mustard on the top half of each roll.
Close the sandwiches by placing the top half of the roll over the layered ingredients.
Spread butter on the outside of each sandwich.
Place the sandwiches on the preheated griddle or panini press.
Grill for 3-4 minutes on each side, or until the bread is toasted, and the cheese is melted.
Remove from heat and let them rest for a minute.
Optionally, cut the sandwiches in half diagonally before serving.

Enjoy this flavorful Cubano, a Cuban sandwich featuring roast pork, ham, Swiss cheese, pickles, and mustard!

Veggie Hummus Wrap

Ingredients:

- 4 whole wheat or spinach tortillas
- 1 cup hummus
- 2 cups mixed salad greens
- 1 cucumber, thinly sliced
- 1 bell pepper, thinly sliced
- 1 medium carrot, julienned
- 1/2 red onion, thinly sliced
- Cherry tomatoes, halved
- Salt and black pepper to taste

Instructions:

Lay out the tortillas on a clean surface.
Spread a generous layer of hummus evenly over each tortilla.
Layer the mixed salad greens, cucumber slices, bell pepper slices, julienned carrot, red onion slices, and cherry tomatoes on each tortilla.
Season with salt and black pepper to taste.
Roll each tortilla tightly into a wrap, ensuring the fillings are enclosed.
Optionally, secure the wraps with toothpicks or wrap them in parchment paper.
Slice the wraps in half diagonally.
Serve immediately and enjoy this nutritious and flavorful Veggie Hummus Wrap!

This wrap is packed with fresh vegetables and creamy hummus, making it a delicious and healthy lunch or snack option.

Philly Cheesesteak Sandwich

Ingredients:

- 4 hoagie rolls
- 1 pound thinly sliced ribeye steak
- 1 large onion, thinly sliced
- 1 large green bell pepper, thinly sliced
- 8 slices provolone cheese
- Salt and black pepper to taste
- Olive oil for cooking

Instructions:

Preheat a skillet or griddle over medium-high heat.
Heat olive oil in the skillet and sauté the sliced onions and bell peppers until softened and slightly caramelized. Remove them from the skillet and set aside.
In the same skillet, add a bit more olive oil if needed and cook the thinly sliced ribeye steak. Season with salt and black pepper to taste. Cook until browned and cooked through.
Once the steak is cooked, mix it with the sautéed onions and bell peppers in the skillet.
Lay out the hoagie rolls and evenly distribute the steak, onion, and pepper mixture on each roll.
Top each sandwich with two slices of provolone cheese.
Optionally, place the sandwiches under the broiler for a minute or two until the cheese is melted and bubbly.
Serve the Philly Cheesesteak Sandwiches hot and enjoy this iconic and savory classic!

Note: You can customize this sandwich with condiments like mayonnaise, ketchup, or hot sauce according to your preference.

Tuna Melt

Ingredients:

- 4 English muffins or your choice of bread
- 2 cans (about 10 ounces each) tuna, drained
- 1/4 cup mayonnaise
- 1 tablespoon Dijon mustard
- 1 celery stalk, finely chopped
- 1/4 red onion, finely chopped
- Salt and black pepper to taste
- 4 slices cheddar or Swiss cheese

Instructions:

Preheat your oven broiler.
In a mixing bowl, combine the drained tuna, mayonnaise, Dijon mustard, chopped celery, and red onion. Mix well until all ingredients are evenly incorporated.
Season the tuna mixture with salt and black pepper to taste.
Split the English muffins and place them on a baking sheet.
Divide the tuna mixture evenly among the English muffin halves, spreading it out.
Top each with a slice of cheddar or Swiss cheese.
Place the baking sheet under the broiler for 2-3 minutes, or until the cheese is melted and bubbly.
Remove from the oven and let them cool for a moment.
Serve the Tuna Melt open-faced and enjoy this delicious and quick-to-make sandwich!

Note: You can customize your Tuna Melt with additional toppings like sliced tomatoes, avocado, or a sprinkle of fresh herbs if desired.

Egg Salad Sandwich

Ingredients:

- 8 large eggs, hard-boiled and peeled
- 1/2 cup mayonnaise
- 1 tablespoon Dijon mustard
- 2 green onions, finely chopped
- 1 celery stalk, finely chopped
- Salt and black pepper to taste
- 8 slices bread (white, whole wheat, or your preference)
- Lettuce leaves (optional)

Instructions:

In a large bowl, chop the hard-boiled eggs into small pieces.
Add mayonnaise, Dijon mustard, chopped green onions, and chopped celery to the bowl. Mix well until all ingredients are combined.
Season the egg salad mixture with salt and black pepper to taste. Adjust the seasoning according to your preference.
Toast the bread slices if desired.
Spread a generous amount of the egg salad mixture onto one side of each bread slice.
Optionally, add lettuce leaves on top of the egg salad.
Top with another slice of bread to create a sandwich.
Slice the sandwiches diagonally and serve immediately.
Enjoy this classic Egg Salad Sandwich that's simple, creamy, and full of flavor!

Pesto Chicken Panini

Ingredients:

- 4 boneless, skinless chicken breasts
- Salt and black pepper to taste
- 1 cup pesto sauce (store-bought or homemade)
- 8 slices mozzarella cheese
- 8 slices ciabatta bread or your choice of panini bread
- Olive oil for brushing

Instructions:

Preheat a grill or grill pan over medium-high heat.
Season the chicken breasts with salt and black pepper.
Grill the chicken breasts until fully cooked, about 6-8 minutes per side, depending on thickness. Ensure the internal temperature reaches 165°F (74°C).
While the chicken is grilling, spread pesto sauce on one side of each slice of bread.
Once the chicken is cooked, place a grilled chicken breast on four slices of bread with the pesto side facing up.
Top each chicken breast with two slices of mozzarella cheese.
Place the remaining slices of bread on top, pesto side down.
Brush the outer sides of the sandwiches with olive oil.
Heat a panini press or a grill pan over medium heat.
Place the sandwiches in the panini press or grill pan and cook until the bread is golden brown, and the cheese is melted, about 3-4 minutes.
Slice the Pesto Chicken Panini diagonally and serve hot.
Enjoy this flavorful and grilled sandwich with a perfect balance of pesto and melted cheese!

Mediterranean Veggie Sandwich

Ingredients:

- 1 large ciabatta loaf or your choice of bread
- 1/2 cup hummus
- 1 medium eggplant, sliced
- 1 large zucchini, sliced
- 1 red bell pepper, sliced
- 1 yellow bell pepper, sliced
- 1 cup cherry tomatoes, halved
- 1/4 cup Kalamata olives, sliced
- 1/4 cup feta cheese, crumbled
- Fresh basil leaves
- Olive oil for grilling
- Salt and black pepper to taste

Instructions:

Preheat a grill or grill pan over medium-high heat.
Brush the eggplant, zucchini, red bell pepper, and yellow bell pepper slices with olive oil. Season with salt and black pepper.
Grill the vegetables until they are tender and have grill marks, about 3-4 minutes per side.
While grilling, slice the ciabatta loaf lengthwise and spread hummus on both halves.
Arrange the grilled vegetables on the bottom half of the ciabatta.
Top with cherry tomatoes, Kalamata olives, crumbled feta cheese, and fresh basil leaves.
Place the other half of the ciabatta on top, pressing gently to create the sandwich.
Optionally, cut the Mediterranean Veggie Sandwich into individual portions.
Serve immediately and savor the delightful flavors of this colorful and wholesome sandwich!

Spicy Chicken Avocado Wrap

Ingredients:

- 1 lb boneless, skinless chicken breasts, grilled and sliced
- 1 teaspoon cayenne pepper
- 1 teaspoon smoked paprika
- 1 teaspoon garlic powder
- Salt and black pepper to taste
- 4 large tortillas (whole wheat or spinach)
- 1 cup cherry tomatoes, halved
- 1 avocado, sliced
- 1/2 cup red onion, thinly sliced
- 1 cup mixed greens (arugula, spinach, or your choice)
- 1/4 cup Greek yogurt or sour cream (optional, for topping)
- Lime wedges for serving

Instructions:

In a bowl, mix cayenne pepper, smoked paprika, garlic powder, salt, and black pepper. Rub this spice mixture onto the grilled and sliced chicken breasts.

Heat the tortillas according to package instructions or warm them on a dry skillet for a few seconds on each side.

Place the spiced chicken slices in the center of each tortilla.

Top the chicken with cherry tomatoes, avocado slices, red onion, and mixed greens.

Optionally, drizzle Greek yogurt or sour cream over the ingredients.

Squeeze lime wedges over the filling for added zest.

Fold the sides of the tortilla over the filling, then roll tightly to form a wrap.

Cut the wraps in half diagonally.

Serve the Spicy Chicken Avocado Wraps immediately, and enjoy the burst of flavors in every bite!

French Dip Sandwich

Ingredients:

For the Roast Beef:

- 3 lbs beef chuck roast
- 2 tablespoons vegetable oil
- 1 onion, sliced
- 3 cloves garlic, minced
- 1 cup beef broth
- 1/2 cup red wine (optional)
- 2 tablespoons Worcestershire sauce
- 1 teaspoon dried thyme
- Salt and black pepper to taste

For the Sandwich:

- French rolls or baguettes
- Provolone or Swiss cheese slices
- Butter for toasting
- Au jus (juices from the roast beef cooking liquid)

Instructions:

Preheat your oven to 325°F (163°C).
Season the chuck roast with salt and black pepper.
Heat vegetable oil in a large oven-safe pot over medium-high heat. Sear the roast on all sides until browned.
Add sliced onions and minced garlic to the pot, cooking until softened.
Pour in beef broth, red wine (if using), Worcestershire sauce, and dried thyme. Bring the liquid to a simmer.
Cover the pot and transfer it to the preheated oven. Roast for about 3 hours or until the beef is tender and easily shreds.
Remove the roast from the pot, shred the beef with two forks, and set aside.
Strain the cooking liquid to create au jus for dipping.
Slice the French rolls or baguettes and butter the cut sides. Toast them under a broiler until golden brown.
Layer the shredded beef on one side of the bread and top with cheese slices.

Place the sandwiches under the broiler again to melt the cheese.
Serve the French Dip Sandwiches with a side of au jus for dipping.
Enjoy the savory goodness of this classic sandwich!

BBQ Pulled Pork Sandwich

Ingredients:

For the Pulled Pork:

- 3 lbs pork shoulder or butt, trimmed
- 1 tablespoon olive oil
- 1 onion, finely chopped
- 3 cloves garlic, minced
- 1 cup barbecue sauce
- 1/2 cup apple cider vinegar
- 1/4 cup brown sugar
- 1 tablespoon Dijon mustard
- 1 teaspoon smoked paprika
- 1 teaspoon cayenne pepper (adjust to taste)
- Salt and black pepper to taste

For the Sandwich:

- Hamburger buns or your preferred sandwich rolls
- Coleslaw (optional, for topping)

Instructions:

Preheat your oven to 325°F (163°C).
Season the pork shoulder or butt with salt and black pepper.
In an oven-safe pot or Dutch oven, heat olive oil over medium-high heat. Sear the pork on all sides until browned.
Add chopped onions and garlic to the pot, cooking until softened.
In a bowl, mix barbecue sauce, apple cider vinegar, brown sugar, Dijon mustard, smoked paprika, and cayenne pepper.
Pour the barbecue sauce mixture over the seared pork.
Cover the pot and transfer it to the preheated oven. Roast for 3-4 hours or until the pork is tender and easily shreds.
Remove the pork from the pot, shred it with two forks, and mix it with the sauce.
Toast the hamburger buns or rolls.

Spoon the pulled pork onto the bottom half of each bun.
Optionally, top with coleslaw for a crunchy contrast.
Place the other half of the bun on top and serve the BBQ Pulled Pork Sandwiches.
Enjoy the smoky, savory flavor of this classic barbecue favorite!

Smoked Salmon Bagel Sandwich

Ingredients:

- 4 bagels, sliced and toasted
- 8 oz smoked salmon
- 1/2 cup cream cheese, softened
- 1 tablespoon capers, drained
- Red onion, thinly sliced
- Fresh dill, for garnish
- Lemon wedges, for serving

Instructions:

Spread a generous layer of softened cream cheese on each half of the toasted bagels.
Lay slices of smoked salmon on the bottom half of the bagels.
Sprinkle capers over the salmon and add thinly sliced red onion.
Garnish with fresh dill on top.
Squeeze a bit of lemon juice over the salmon for a burst of citrus flavor.
Place the other half of the bagel on top to create a sandwich.
Serve the Smoked Salmon Bagel Sandwiches immediately.
Enjoy the delightful combination of creamy cheese, smoky salmon, and zesty toppings!

Roast Beef and Horseradish Wrap

Ingredients:

- 1 lb thinly sliced roast beef
- 4 large tortillas or wraps
- 1/2 cup horseradish sauce
- 1 cup arugula or mixed greens
- 1 red onion, thinly sliced
- 1 cup cherry tomatoes, halved
- Salt and black pepper to taste

Instructions:

Lay out the tortillas or wraps on a clean surface.
Spread a generous layer of horseradish sauce over each tortilla.
Evenly distribute the roast beef slices on top of the horseradish sauce.
Add a handful of arugula or mixed greens to each wrap.
Scatter thinly sliced red onions and halved cherry tomatoes over the greens.
Season with salt and black pepper to taste.
Roll up each tortilla tightly, forming a wrap.
Slice the wraps in half diagonally for easy serving.
Serve the Roast Beef and Horseradish Wraps immediately.
Enjoy the bold flavors of roast beef paired with the zing of horseradish in this satisfying wrap!

Chickpea Salad Sandwich (Vegan)

Ingredients:

- 1 can (15 oz) chickpeas, drained and rinsed
- 1/4 cup vegan mayonnaise
- 1 tablespoon Dijon mustard
- 1 celery stalk, finely chopped
- 1/4 red onion, finely chopped
- 1 tablespoon fresh lemon juice
- 1 teaspoon agave syrup or maple syrup
- Salt and black pepper to taste
- Bread slices or rolls
- Lettuce leaves and tomato slices for garnish

Instructions:

In a bowl, mash the chickpeas using a fork or potato masher.
Add vegan mayonnaise, Dijon mustard, chopped celery, chopped red onion, lemon juice, and agave syrup to the mashed chickpeas.
Mix well until all ingredients are combined.
Season with salt and black pepper to taste. Adjust the seasonings as needed.
Spread a generous layer of the chickpea salad onto bread slices or rolls.
Top with lettuce leaves and tomato slices.
Place another slice of bread on top to create a sandwich.
Repeat for additional sandwiches.
Serve the Chickpea Salad Sandwiches immediately.
Enjoy this vegan twist on a classic chicken salad sandwich, packed with protein and flavor!

Italian Submarine Sandwich

Ingredients:

- 1 large Italian sub roll or baguette
- 4 oz thinly sliced ham
- 4 oz thinly sliced salami
- 4 oz thinly sliced pepperoni
- 4 slices provolone cheese
- 1/2 cup shredded iceberg lettuce
- 1/4 cup sliced black olives
- 1/4 cup sliced banana peppers
- 1/4 cup diced red onions
- 1/4 cup diced tomatoes
- Salt and black pepper to taste
- Olive oil and red wine vinegar for drizzling
- Italian seasoning for seasoning

Instructions:

Slice the Italian sub roll or baguette horizontally, creating a top and bottom.
Layer the ham, salami, and pepperoni evenly on the bottom half of the bread.
Place provolone cheese slices on top of the meat.
In a bowl, mix shredded lettuce, black olives, banana peppers, red onions, and diced tomatoes.
Season the vegetable mixture with salt, black pepper, and a sprinkle of Italian seasoning.
Spoon the vegetable mixture over the cheese layer.
Drizzle olive oil and red wine vinegar over the vegetable layer.
Place the top half of the bread on the sandwich, pressing down gently.
Slice the Italian Submarine Sandwich into individual servings.
Serve immediately and savor the delicious layers of Italian flavors in every bite!

Chicken Shawarma Wrap

Ingredients:

For Marinating the Chicken:

- 1 lb boneless, skinless chicken thighs, thinly sliced
- 3 cloves garlic, minced
- 1 teaspoon ground cumin
- 1 teaspoon ground coriander
- 1 teaspoon ground paprika
- 1 teaspoon ground turmeric
- 1 teaspoon ground cinnamon
- 1/4 teaspoon cayenne pepper
- Salt and black pepper to taste
- 2 tablespoons plain yogurt
- 2 tablespoons olive oil
- Juice of 1 lemon

For Garlic Sauce:

- 1/2 cup tahini
- 2 cloves garlic, minced
- 2 tablespoons lemon juice
- 2 tablespoons water
- Salt to taste

For Assembling the Wrap:

- Flatbreads or wraps
- Sliced tomatoes
- Sliced cucumbers
- Sliced red onions
- Fresh parsley, chopped

Instructions:

In a bowl, mix together all the marinade ingredients: minced garlic, cumin, coriander, paprika, turmeric, cinnamon, cayenne pepper, salt, black pepper, yogurt, olive oil, and lemon juice.

Add the sliced chicken thighs to the marinade, making sure each piece is well-coated. Cover and refrigerate for at least 1-2 hours, or overnight for more flavor.

Preheat a grill or grill pan over medium-high heat. Cook the marinated chicken slices until fully cooked and slightly charred, about 5-7 minutes per side.

While the chicken is cooking, prepare the garlic sauce. In a small bowl, whisk together tahini, minced garlic, lemon juice, water, and salt until smooth.

Warm the flatbreads or wraps.

Assemble the wraps by placing a generous portion of the grilled chicken on each flatbread. Top with sliced tomatoes, cucumbers, red onions, and fresh parsley. Drizzle the garlic sauce over the filling.

Fold the sides of the flatbread over the filling and roll up tightly to create a wrap. Secure with toothpicks if needed.

Serve the Chicken Shawarma Wraps immediately and enjoy the delicious, flavorful taste of this Middle Eastern classic!

California Turkey Club Wrap

Ingredients:

- 4 large tortillas or wraps
- 1 lb cooked turkey breast, sliced
- 8 slices bacon, cooked crisp
- 1 large avocado, sliced
- 1 cup cherry tomatoes, halved
- 1 cup lettuce, shredded
- 1/2 cup mayonnaise
- 1 tablespoon Dijon mustard
- Salt and black pepper to taste

Instructions:

In a small bowl, mix mayonnaise and Dijon mustard. Season with salt and black pepper to taste.
Lay out the tortillas on a clean surface.
Spread the mayonnaise and mustard mixture evenly over each tortilla.
Arrange sliced turkey, bacon, avocado, cherry tomatoes, and shredded lettuce in the center of each tortilla.
Fold the sides of the tortilla over the filling and roll tightly to create a wrap.
Secure with toothpicks if needed.
Slice the wraps in half diagonally.
Serve the California Turkey Club Wraps immediately, and enjoy a delightful combination of flavors and textures!

Grilled Cheese with Tomato Soup

Ingredients:

For Grilled Cheese:

- 8 slices of bread (white or whole wheat)
- 8 slices of cheddar cheese
- Butter for spreading

For Tomato Soup:

- 1 can (28 oz) crushed tomatoes
- 1 onion, finely chopped
- 2 cloves garlic, minced
- 2 cups vegetable broth
- 1 teaspoon dried basil
- 1 teaspoon dried oregano
- 1/2 teaspoon sugar
- Salt and black pepper to taste
- 1/2 cup heavy cream (optional, for a creamier soup)

Instructions:

For Grilled Cheese:

Lay out the bread slices and place a slice of cheddar cheese between two slices, creating four sandwiches.
Spread butter on the outer side of each sandwich.
Heat a skillet or griddle over medium heat.
Place the sandwiches on the skillet and cook until the bread is golden brown and the cheese is melted, about 3-4 minutes per side.
Remove from the skillet and let them cool slightly before slicing.

For Tomato Soup:

In a large pot, sauté the chopped onion in olive oil until translucent.

Add minced garlic and cook for an additional minute.
Pour in the crushed tomatoes and vegetable broth.
Stir in dried basil, dried oregano, sugar, salt, and black pepper.
Bring the soup to a simmer and let it cook for about 15-20 minutes, allowing the flavors to meld.
If desired, stir in heavy cream for a creamier texture.
Use an immersion blender to puree the soup until smooth. Alternatively, transfer the soup to a blender in batches and blend until smooth. Be cautious, as the soup will be hot.
Adjust seasoning to taste.
Serve the Grilled Cheese alongside a warm bowl of Tomato Soup, creating a classic and comforting combination. Enjoy!

Turkey Cranberry Panini

Ingredients:

- 8 slices of sourdough bread
- 1/2 cup cranberry sauce
- 1 pound roasted turkey, sliced
- 8 slices provolone cheese
- 1/4 cup mayonnaise
- 2 tablespoons Dijon mustard
- Butter for spreading

Instructions:

In a small bowl, mix mayonnaise and Dijon mustard.
Lay out the slices of sourdough bread.
Spread the mayonnaise and mustard mixture evenly on one side of each slice.
On half of the slices, layer turkey, provolone cheese, and cranberry sauce.
Top with the remaining slices of bread, mayo-mustard side down, creating sandwiches.
Heat a panini press or a skillet over medium heat.
Spread butter on the outer side of each sandwich.
Place the sandwiches on the panini press or skillet and cook until the bread is golden brown, and the cheese is melted, about 3-4 minutes per side.
Remove from the press or skillet, let them cool for a moment, and slice diagonally.
Serve the Turkey Cranberry Panini warm, combining the savory turkey with the sweet and tangy cranberry sauce for a delightful flavor contrast. Enjoy!

Shrimp Po' Boy Sandwich

Ingredients:

For the Shrimp:

- 1 pound large shrimp, peeled and deveined
- 1 cup buttermilk
- 1 cup cornmeal
- 1 cup all-purpose flour
- 1 teaspoon paprika
- 1 teaspoon garlic powder
- Salt and black pepper to taste
- Vegetable oil for frying

For the Remoulade Sauce:

- 1 cup mayonnaise
- 2 tablespoons Dijon mustard
- 1 tablespoon hot sauce
- 1 tablespoon capers, chopped
- 2 green onions, finely chopped
- 1 tablespoon fresh parsley, chopped
- Salt and black pepper to taste

For the Sandwich:

- 4 French baguettes or sub rolls
- Shredded lettuce
- Sliced tomatoes
- Sliced dill pickles

Instructions:

For the Shrimp:

In a bowl, marinate the shrimp in buttermilk for at least 30 minutes.

In another bowl, mix cornmeal, flour, paprika, garlic powder, salt, and black pepper.

Heat vegetable oil in a deep fryer or large skillet to 350°F (175°C).

Dredge each shrimp in the cornmeal mixture, ensuring they are well-coated.

Fry the shrimp in batches until golden brown and cooked through, about 2-3 minutes per batch.

Remove the shrimp with a slotted spoon and let them drain on paper towels.

For the Remoulade Sauce:

In a small bowl, whisk together mayonnaise, Dijon mustard, hot sauce, capers, green onions, parsley, salt, and black pepper.

Refrigerate the remoulade sauce until ready to use.

Assembling the Sandwich:

Slice the French baguettes or sub rolls lengthwise.

Spread a generous amount of remoulade sauce on the insides of each roll.

Layer shredded lettuce, sliced tomatoes, and dill pickles on the bottom half of each roll.

Place a generous amount of fried shrimp on top of the vegetables.

Top with the other half of the roll and press down gently.

Serve the Shrimp Po' Boy Sandwiches immediately, capturing the flavors of crispy shrimp and zesty remoulade in every bite. Enjoy!

Buffalo Chicken Wrap

Ingredients:

For the Buffalo Chicken:

- 1 pound boneless, skinless chicken breasts, cooked and shredded
- 1/2 cup buffalo sauce
- 2 tablespoons unsalted butter, melted
- 1 teaspoon garlic powder
- Salt and black pepper to taste

For the Wrap:

- 4 large flour tortillas
- 1 cup shredded lettuce
- 1 cup diced tomatoes
- 1 cup shredded cheddar cheese
- 1/2 cup blue cheese dressing
- 1/4 cup chopped green onions (optional)
- Ranch or additional buffalo sauce for drizzling (optional)

Instructions:

For the Buffalo Chicken:

In a bowl, combine shredded chicken with buffalo sauce, melted butter, garlic powder, salt, and black pepper. Toss until the chicken is well coated.
Heat a skillet over medium heat and warm the buffalo chicken mixture for 3-5 minutes, stirring occasionally. Remove from heat.

For the Wrap:

Lay out the flour tortillas on a clean surface.
Divide the shredded lettuce, diced tomatoes, and shredded cheddar cheese evenly among the tortillas.

Spoon the warm buffalo chicken mixture over the vegetables and cheese on each tortilla.
Drizzle blue cheese dressing over the chicken.
If desired, sprinkle chopped green onions over the top.
Roll up each tortilla tightly to form a wrap.
Optionally, drizzle with additional ranch or buffalo sauce.
Slice the Buffalo Chicken Wraps in half diagonally and serve immediately.

Enjoy your Buffalo Chicken Wraps! They're perfect for a quick and tasty meal.

Avocado and Bacon Grilled Cheese

Ingredients:

- 8 slices of bread (your choice, but a hearty bread works well)
- 2 ripe avocados, sliced
- 8 slices of cooked bacon
- 2 cups shredded cheese (cheddar, mozzarella, or a blend)
- Butter for spreading

Instructions:

Prep the Ingredients:
- Cook the bacon until crispy. Set aside on paper towels to drain excess grease.
- Slice the avocados and shred the cheese.

Assemble the Sandwiches:
- Lay out 8 slices of bread on a clean surface.
- On 4 of the slices, layer shredded cheese, sliced avocado, and cooked bacon.
- Top each with another slice of bread to form sandwiches.

Grill the Sandwiches:
- Heat a skillet or griddle over medium heat.
- Spread butter on one side of each sandwich.
- Place the sandwiches, buttered side down, on the hot surface.
- Cook until the bread is golden brown and the cheese is melted, about 3-4 minutes per side.

Serve:
- Remove the sandwiches from the skillet and let them cool for a minute.
- Optionally, slice each sandwich in half diagonally for serving.

Enjoy:
- Serve your Avocado and Bacon Grilled Cheese sandwiches warm and enjoy the creamy avocado, crispy bacon, and gooey melted cheese.

This Avocado and Bacon Grilled Cheese is a delightful twist on the classic sandwich, adding richness and flavor with avocado and bacon.

Chicken Pesto Ciabatta

Ingredients:

- 1 pound boneless, skinless chicken breasts
- Salt and black pepper, to taste
- 1 tablespoon olive oil
- 1 loaf of ciabatta bread, sliced
- 1/2 cup basil pesto (store-bought or homemade)
- 1 cup cherry tomatoes, halved
- 1 cup fresh mozzarella, sliced
- Fresh basil leaves for garnish (optional)

Instructions:

For the Chicken:

Preheat your grill or grill pan over medium-high heat.
Season the chicken breasts with salt and black pepper.
Brush the chicken with olive oil to prevent sticking on the grill.
Grill the chicken for about 6-8 minutes per side or until fully cooked. The internal temperature should reach 165°F (74°C).
Remove the chicken from the grill and let it rest for a few minutes. Slice the chicken into thin strips.

Assembling the Ciabatta:

Preheat your oven to a broil setting.
Place the ciabatta slices on a baking sheet.
Spread a generous layer of basil pesto on each slice of ciabatta.
Top with sliced grilled chicken, halved cherry tomatoes, and fresh mozzarella.
Place the baking sheet under the broiler for 2-3 minutes or until the cheese is melted and bubbly.
Remove from the oven and garnish with fresh basil leaves if desired.
Serve the Chicken Pesto Ciabatta warm. You can also drizzle a little extra pesto on top for added flavor.

Enjoy your delicious Chicken Pesto Ciabatta! It's a perfect combination of grilled chicken, vibrant pesto, and gooey mozzarella on crusty ciabatta bread.

Classic Peanut Butter and Jelly

Ingredients:

- 2 slices of your favorite bread (white, wheat, or whole grain)
- 2 tablespoons peanut butter
- 1-2 tablespoons jelly or jam (grape, strawberry, or your preferred flavor)

Instructions:

Spread Peanut Butter:
- Take one slice of bread and spread a generous layer of peanut butter evenly over the entire surface.

Add Jelly or Jam:
- On the second slice of bread, spread an even layer of jelly or jam. You can use the same knife or a different one to keep the flavors separate.

Combine and Press:
- Press the two slices of bread together, peanut butter side facing the jelly side, creating a sandwich.

Optional: Cut or Leave Whole:
- You can choose to leave the sandwich whole or cut it into halves or quarters.

Serve and Enjoy:
- Your classic Peanut Butter and Jelly sandwich is ready to be enjoyed! It's a perfect quick and easy meal or snack.

Feel free to customize by using different types of bread, nut butter variations, or experimenting with unique jams and jellies to suit your taste preferences.

Gyro Sandwich with Tzatziki Sauce

Ingredients:

For Gyro:

- 1 pound thinly sliced lamb or chicken (pre-cooked or raw)
- 1 tablespoon olive oil
- 1 teaspoon dried oregano

- 1 teaspoon ground cumin
- 1 teaspoon paprika
- Salt and pepper to taste
- Pita bread or flatbreads

For Tzatziki Sauce:

- 1 cup Greek yogurt
- 1 cucumber, grated and drained
- 2 cloves garlic, minced
- 1 tablespoon fresh dill, chopped
- 1 tablespoon fresh mint, chopped
- 1 tablespoon lemon juice
- Salt and pepper to taste

For Garnish:

- Sliced tomatoes
- Sliced red onions
- Lettuce

Instructions:

Prepare Gyro Meat:
- If using raw meat, marinate it in olive oil, oregano, cumin, paprika, salt, and pepper. Cook in a skillet until fully cooked and slightly crispy.

Make Tzatziki Sauce:
- In a bowl, combine Greek yogurt, grated cucumber (squeeze out excess water), minced garlic, chopped dill, chopped mint, lemon juice, salt, and pepper. Mix well and refrigerate.

Warm Pita Bread:
- Warm the pita bread in a skillet or microwave until soft and pliable.

Assemble Gyro Sandwich:
- Place a generous amount of gyro meat onto the pita bread.
- Add sliced tomatoes, red onions, and lettuce.
- Drizzle a generous amount of tzatziki sauce over the top.

Fold and Serve:
- Fold the pita in half or roll it up, securing it with parchment paper or foil if needed.

Enjoy:
- Your delicious Gyro Sandwich with Tzatziki Sauce is ready to be enjoyed! Serve it with extra sauce on the side for dipping.

Feel free to customize your Gyro Sandwich with additional toppings like feta cheese, olives, or hot sauce according to your preferences.

Smashed Chickpea Avocado Sandwich (Vegan)

Ingredients:

For the Smashed Chickpea Mixture:

- 1 can (15 oz) chickpeas, drained and rinsed
- 1 ripe avocado
- 1 tablespoon lemon juice
- 2 tablespoons fresh cilantro, chopped
- Salt and pepper to taste

For the Sandwich:

- Bread slices (your choice of type)
- Lettuce leaves
- Tomato slices
- Red onion slices (optional)

Instructions:

Prepare Smashed Chickpea Mixture:
- In a bowl, combine the drained chickpeas and ripe avocado.
- Use a fork to smash the chickpeas and avocado together until well combined, leaving some texture.
- Add lemon juice, chopped cilantro, salt, and pepper. Mix well.

Assemble the Sandwich:
- Take a slice of bread and spread a generous amount of the smashed chickpea mixture.

Add Toppings:
- Layer on lettuce leaves, tomato slices, and red onion slices if desired.

Top with Another Slice of Bread:
- Place another slice of bread on top to create a sandwich.

Slice and Serve:
- If desired, slice the sandwich in half diagonally or as desired.

Enjoy:

- Your Smashed Chickpea Avocado Sandwich is ready to be enjoyed! It's a delicious and satisfying vegan option.

Feel free to customize the sandwich with additional toppings like sprouts, cucumber slices, or your favorite vegan condiments.

Monte Cristo Sandwich

Ingredients:

- 8 slices of bread (white or whole wheat)
- 4 slices of ham
- 4 slices of turkey
- 4 slices of Swiss cheese
- 3 large eggs
- 1/2 cup milk
- Salt and pepper to taste
- 2 tablespoons Dijon mustard
- Powdered sugar for dusting
- Raspberry or strawberry jam for serving

Instructions:

Assemble the Sandwiches:
- Lay out 4 slices of bread. On each slice, layer a slice of ham, a slice of turkey, and a slice of Swiss cheese. Top each with another slice of bread to create 4 sandwiches.

Prepare the Egg Mixture:
- In a shallow dish, whisk together eggs, milk, salt, and pepper.

Dip the Sandwiches:
- Carefully dip each sandwich into the egg mixture, making sure both sides are well-coated.

Cook the Sandwiches:
- In a large skillet or griddle, melt butter over medium heat. Place the dipped sandwiches on the skillet and cook until golden brown on each side, about 3-4 minutes per side.

Serve:
- Remove the sandwiches from the skillet and let them rest for a minute.
- Dust the sandwiches with powdered sugar.
- Serve with a side of Dijon mustard and raspberry or strawberry jam for dipping.

Enjoy:
- Your Monte Cristo Sandwiches are ready to be enjoyed! Serve them warm and savor the delicious combination of savory and sweet flavors.

Feel free to adjust the ingredients or add your favorite variations, such as adding a touch of honey to the Dijon mustard or using different types of bread.

Turkey Apple Cheddar Panini

Ingredients:

- 8 slices of artisan bread
- 1/2 cup Dijon mustard
- 8 slices of roasted turkey breast
- 1 large apple, thinly sliced
- 8 slices of sharp cheddar cheese
- 1/4 cup mayonnaise
- 4 tablespoons unsalted butter, softened

Instructions:

Prepare the Spread:
- In a small bowl, mix Dijon mustard and mayonnaise to create a spread.

Assemble the Panini:
- Lay out 8 slices of bread. On one side of each slice, spread the Dijon-mayo mixture.

Layer Ingredients:
- On half of the bread slices (spread side up), layer slices of turkey, apple, and cheddar cheese.

Create Sandwiches:
- Top each with the remaining slices of bread (spread side down), creating sandwiches.

Butter the Bread:
- Spread softened butter on the outer sides of each sandwich.

Cook the Panini:
- Heat a panini press or a skillet over medium heat. If using a skillet, press the sandwiches down with a spatula.
- Cook each side until the bread is golden brown, and the cheese is melted, about 3-4 minutes per side.

Slice and Serve:
- Remove the panini from the press or skillet and let them cool for a moment.
- Slice the sandwiches diagonally and serve immediately.

Enjoy:

- Your Turkey Apple Cheddar Panini is ready to be enjoyed! The combination of savory turkey, sweet apple, and melted cheddar makes for a delightful sandwich.

Feel free to customize with your favorite bread or add a touch of honey or cranberry sauce for an extra layer of flavor.

Banh Mi Sandwich

Ingredients:

- Baguette or French bread rolls
- 1/2 pound pork belly or chicken, thinly sliced
- 1 tablespoon soy sauce
- 1 tablespoon fish sauce
- 1 tablespoon honey
- 2 cloves garlic, minced
- 1 tablespoon vegetable oil
- 1 cup pickled daikon and carrots
- Fresh cilantro leaves
- Fresh jalapeño slices
- Mayonnaise or aioli
- Hoisin sauce (optional)

Instructions:

Marinate the Meat:
- In a bowl, combine soy sauce, fish sauce, honey, minced garlic, and vegetable oil. Marinate the sliced pork belly or chicken in this mixture for at least 30 minutes.

Cook the Meat:
- Grill or pan-fry the marinated meat until it's fully cooked and has a nice caramelized exterior.

Prepare the Baguette:
- Cut the baguette or French bread rolls in half lengthwise.

Assemble the Banh Mi:
- Spread a layer of mayonnaise or aioli on one or both sides of the bread.
- Place the grilled pork belly or chicken on the bread.

Add Toppings:
- Top with pickled daikon and carrots, fresh cilantro leaves, and jalapeño slices. Add hoisin sauce if desired.

Press and Serve:
- Press the sandwich together and serve immediately.

Enjoy:

- The Banh Mi sandwich is ready to be enjoyed! The combination of savory, sweet, tangy, and spicy flavors makes it a delightful Vietnamese-inspired treat.

Feel free to customize with your favorite proteins or add additional toppings like cucumber slices for a refreshing crunch.

Portobello Mushroom Burger (Vegetarian)

Ingredients:

- 4 large portobello mushrooms, stems removed
- 1/4 cup balsamic vinegar
- 2 tablespoons olive oil
- 2 cloves garlic, minced
- 1 teaspoon dried thyme
- Salt and black pepper to taste
- 4 whole-grain burger buns
- 1 cup arugula or spinach
- 1 large tomato, sliced
- 1 red onion, thinly sliced
- 4 slices Swiss or your favorite cheese (optional)
- Mayonnaise or your preferred sauce

Instructions:

Marinate the Mushrooms:
- In a bowl, whisk together balsamic vinegar, olive oil, minced garlic, dried thyme, salt, and black pepper. Place the portobello mushrooms in a shallow dish and pour the marinade over them. Let them marinate for at least 30 minutes, turning occasionally.

Grill or Cook the Mushrooms:
- Preheat your grill or a grill pan over medium heat. Grill the marinated mushrooms for about 4-5 minutes per side or until they are tender and cooked through. Optionally, add a slice of cheese on top during the last minute of cooking.

Prepare the Buns:
- Toast the whole-grain burger buns on the grill or in a toaster until lightly golden.

Assemble the Burgers:
- Spread mayonnaise or your preferred sauce on the bottom half of each bun.
- Place a grilled portobello mushroom on each bun.
- Top with arugula or spinach, tomato slices, and red onion slices.

Serve:

- Place the top half of the bun on each assembled burger.

Enjoy:
- Your Portobello Mushroom Burger is ready to be served. Enjoy this hearty and flavorful vegetarian alternative!

Feel free to customize your burger with additional toppings such as avocado, pickles, or your favorite condiments.

Spicy Italian Sausage Sub

Ingredients:

- 4 Italian sausage links (spicy or mild)
- 4 sub rolls or baguettes
- 1 cup marinara sauce
- 1 bell pepper, thinly sliced
- 1 onion, thinly sliced
- 1 teaspoon dried oregano
- 1 teaspoon dried basil
- 1/2 teaspoon red pepper flakes (adjust to taste)
- Salt and black pepper to taste
- 1 cup shredded mozzarella cheese
- Olive oil for cooking

Instructions:

Cook the Sausages:
- Preheat a skillet or grill pan over medium heat. Cook the Italian sausages until browned and cooked through, turning occasionally. This usually takes about 15-20 minutes.

Prepare the Vegetables:
- In the same skillet, add a bit of olive oil if needed. Add thinly sliced bell peppers and onions. Sauté until they are tender and slightly caramelized.

Season and Simmer:
- Add dried oregano, dried basil, red pepper flakes, salt, and black pepper to the sautéed vegetables. Pour in the marinara sauce and let it simmer for 5-7 minutes until the flavors meld.

Assemble the Subs:
- Preheat your oven's broiler. Slice the sub rolls or baguettes and place them on a baking sheet.
- Split the sausages lengthwise and arrange them on the bread. Spoon the sautéed vegetables and marinara sauce over the sausages.

Add Cheese and Broil:
- Sprinkle shredded mozzarella cheese over the top of each sub. Place the baking sheet under the broiler until the cheese is melted and bubbly, usually 2-3 minutes.

Serve Hot:
- Remove from the oven and let the subs cool slightly before serving.

Enjoy:
- Your Spicy Italian Sausage Subs are ready to be enjoyed. Serve with extra marinara sauce or your favorite condiments.

Feel free to customize your subs with additional toppings like olives, banana peppers, or a drizzle of balsamic glaze.

Chicken Caesar Salad Wrap

Ingredients:

- 2 boneless, skinless chicken breasts
- Salt and black pepper to taste
- 1 tablespoon olive oil
- 4 large whole wheat or spinach tortillas
- 2 cups Romaine lettuce, chopped
- 1 cup cherry tomatoes, halved
- 1/2 cup grated Parmesan cheese
- Caesar dressing (store-bought or homemade)
- Croutons for crunch (optional)

Instructions:

Season and Cook Chicken:
- Season chicken breasts with salt and black pepper. In a skillet over medium heat, add olive oil. Cook the chicken breasts until they are no longer pink in the center, about 6-8 minutes per side. Let them rest for a few minutes before slicing.

Prepare Ingredients:
- Chop the Romaine lettuce, halve the cherry tomatoes, and grate the Parmesan cheese. If you're using croutons, set them aside.

Assemble Wraps:
- Lay out the tortillas on a flat surface. Place a portion of the sliced cooked chicken in the center of each tortilla.

Add Salad Components:
- Layer chopped Romaine lettuce, halved cherry tomatoes, and grated Parmesan cheese over the chicken.

Drizzle with Dressing:
- Drizzle Caesar dressing over the salad components. Adjust the amount to your preference.

Optional Crunch:
- If using croutons, sprinkle them over the salad for an added crunch.

Wrap It Up:
- Fold in the sides of the tortilla and then roll it up tightly, creating a wrap.

Serve:

- Slice the wraps in half diagonally and serve immediately.

Enjoy:
- Your Chicken Caesar Salad Wraps are ready to be enjoyed. They make a delicious and portable lunch or dinner option.

Feel free to customize the wraps with additional ingredients like bacon bits, avocado slices, or a sprinkle of black pepper for extra flavor.

Croque Monsieur

Ingredients:

- 8 slices of high-quality white bread
- 4 tablespoons unsalted butter, softened
- 8 slices ham
- 2 cups Gruyère cheese, grated
- Dijon mustard (optional)
- Salt and black pepper to taste
- Bechamel Sauce:
    - 3 tablespoons unsalted butter
    - 3 tablespoons all-purpose flour
    - 2 cups whole milk
    - Salt, pepper, and nutmeg to taste

Instructions:

Make Bechamel Sauce:
- In a saucepan over medium heat, melt the butter. Add flour and whisk continuously for about 2 minutes to create a roux.
- Gradually add the milk, whisking constantly to avoid lumps. Cook until the sauce thickens.
- Season with salt, pepper, and a pinch of nutmeg. Set aside.

Prepare Sandwiches:
- Lay out 8 slices of bread. Spread a thin layer of Dijon mustard on half of the slices if desired.
- Place a slice of ham on each mustard-coated slice, followed by a generous amount of Gruyère cheese.

Assemble Sandwiches:
- Top each sandwich with the remaining slices of bread to create ham and cheese sandwiches.

Butter the Bread:
- Spread a thin layer of softened butter on the outer sides of each sandwich.

Cook the Sandwiches:
- In a skillet over medium heat, cook the sandwiches until golden brown on both sides and the cheese is melted.

Add Bechamel Sauce:

- Preheat the broiler. Transfer the sandwiches to a baking sheet and spoon a generous amount of bechamel sauce over the top of each sandwich.

Broil:
- Place the sandwiches under the broiler for 2-3 minutes or until the bechamel is bubbly and golden.

Serve:
- Remove from the broiler, let them cool for a minute, and then serve hot.

Enjoy:
- Croque Monsieur is best enjoyed warm. Serve with a side salad for a delightful meal.

This classic French sandwich is a decadent treat with its creamy bechamel sauce and gooey Gruyère cheese.

Crab Cake Sandwich

Ingredients:

For Crab Cakes:

- 1 pound lump crabmeat, picked over for shells
- 1/2 cup mayonnaise
- 1 large egg
- 1 tablespoon Dijon mustard
- 1 tablespoon Worcestershire sauce
- 1 teaspoon Old Bay seasoning
- 1 cup breadcrumbs
- 2 tablespoons fresh parsley, chopped
- Salt and pepper to taste
- Olive oil for frying

For Sandwich:

- 4 hamburger buns, toasted
- Lettuce leaves
- Sliced tomatoes
- Pickles (optional)

For Remoulade Sauce:

- 1/2 cup mayonnaise
- 2 tablespoons Dijon mustard
- 1 tablespoon capers, chopped
- 1 tablespoon fresh parsley, chopped
- 1 teaspoon hot sauce
- Salt and pepper to taste

Instructions:

Prepare Crab Cakes:

- In a large bowl, combine crabmeat, mayonnaise, egg, Dijon mustard, Worcestershire sauce, Old Bay seasoning, breadcrumbs, parsley, salt, and pepper. Gently mix until well combined.
- Shape the mixture into crab cakes, about 1/2 cup each.

Fry Crab Cakes:
- Heat olive oil in a skillet over medium heat. Fry crab cakes for 3-4 minutes per side or until golden brown and cooked through.

Make Remoulade Sauce:
- In a small bowl, whisk together mayonnaise, Dijon mustard, capers, parsley, hot sauce, salt, and pepper.

Assemble Sandwiches:
- Spread remoulade sauce on the toasted buns.
- Place a crab cake on the bottom half of each bun.
- Top with lettuce, sliced tomatoes, and pickles if desired.
- Cover with the top bun.

Serve:
- Serve the crab cake sandwiches immediately, and enjoy the delicious flavors.

This Crab Cake Sandwich combines the succulence of crab cakes with a zesty remoulade sauce, creating a mouthwatering seafood delight.

Hawaiian BBQ Chicken Sandwich

Ingredients:

For BBQ Chicken:

- 2 boneless, skinless chicken breasts
- 1 cup pineapple juice
- 1/2 cup soy sauce
- 1/4 cup ketchup
- 2 tablespoons brown sugar
- 2 cloves garlic, minced
- 1 teaspoon ginger, grated
- Salt and pepper to taste
- 4 hamburger buns, toasted

For Toppings:

- Grilled pineapple slices
- Red onion, thinly sliced
- Lettuce leaves

For Sriracha Mayo:

- 1/2 cup mayonnaise
- 1 tablespoon Sriracha sauce (adjust to taste)
- 1 teaspoon lime juice
- Salt and pepper to taste

Instructions:

Marinate Chicken:
- In a bowl, combine pineapple juice, soy sauce, ketchup, brown sugar, minced garlic, grated ginger, salt, and pepper. Mix well.
- Place chicken breasts in a zip-top bag and pour half of the marinade over them. Seal the bag and marinate in the refrigerator for at least 30 minutes (overnight for best flavor).

- Reserve the remaining marinade for basting.

Grill Chicken:
- Preheat the grill to medium-high heat.
- Grill the marinated chicken breasts for 6-8 minutes per side or until fully cooked, basting with the reserved marinade.

Prepare Sriracha Mayo:
- In a small bowl, mix mayonnaise, Sriracha sauce, lime juice, salt, and pepper. Adjust Sriracha to your desired level of spiciness.

Assemble Sandwiches:
- Spread Sriracha mayo on the bottom half of each toasted bun.
- Place grilled chicken on top of the mayo.
- Add grilled pineapple slices, red onion, and lettuce leaves.
- Cover with the top bun.

Serve:
- Serve the Hawaiian BBQ Chicken Sandwiches with your favorite side dishes, and enjoy the tropical flavors.

This Hawaiian BBQ Chicken Sandwich brings the sweetness of pineapple and the heat of Sriracha together for a delightful and flavorful sandwich experience.

The Elvis Sandwich (Peanut Butter, Banana, and Bacon)

Ingredients:

- 2 slices of bread (white or whole wheat)
- 2 tablespoons peanut butter
- 1 ripe banana, sliced
- 2-3 slices of crispy bacon

Instructions:

Cook Bacon:
- Cook the bacon until it's crispy. You can use a skillet on the stovetop or bake it in the oven according to your preference. Drain excess grease on paper towels.

Toast Bread:
- Toast the bread slices to your liking.

Spread Peanut Butter:
- Spread peanut butter evenly on one side of each toasted bread slice.

Assemble Sandwich:
- Place the sliced banana on one of the bread slices, arranging them evenly.
- Lay the crispy bacon slices on top of the banana.

Top and Serve:
- Place the second slice of bread with peanut butter on top, creating a sandwich.
- Press gently to secure the sandwich.

Slice and Enjoy:
- If desired, slice the sandwich in half diagonally.
- Serve and enjoy this unique combination of flavors inspired by Elvis Presley's favorite sandwich.

The Elvis Sandwich, a favorite of the legendary musician Elvis Presley, combines the richness of peanut butter with the sweetness of bananas and the savory crunch of bacon. It's a delightful and unconventional treat that's both satisfying and delicious.

Chipotle Turkey Panini

Ingredients:

- 8 slices of sourdough or ciabatta bread
- 1 pound sliced turkey breast
- 8 slices pepper jack cheese
- 1/2 cup chipotle mayonnaise
- 1 cup fresh spinach leaves
- 1 medium tomato, thinly sliced
- Butter for grilling

Instructions:

Preheat Panini Press:
- Preheat your panini press or sandwich maker.

Assemble Sandwiches:
- Lay out 8 slices of bread.
- On 4 slices, evenly spread chipotle mayonnaise.

Layer Ingredients:
- Place a layer of turkey on the mayonnaise-covered slices.
- Add a slice of pepper jack cheese on top of the turkey.
- Add a few spinach leaves and a couple of tomato slices.

Top and Close:
- Place the remaining 4 slices of bread on top to create sandwiches.

Butter and Grill:
- Lightly butter the outside of each sandwich.
- Place the sandwiches on the preheated panini press and grill until the bread is golden brown, and the cheese is melted.

Serve and Enjoy:
- Remove from the press, slice diagonally if desired, and serve immediately.

Optional:
- Add extra chipotle mayo for dipping or serve with a side of pickles.

The Chipotle Turkey Panini combines smoky chipotle mayo, succulent turkey, melted pepper jack cheese, and fresh veggies, creating a zesty and satisfying grilled sandwich. Perfect for a quick and flavorful meal.

Chicken and Waffle Sandwich

Ingredients:

For the Chicken:

- 4 boneless, skinless chicken breasts
- 1 cup buttermilk
- 1 cup all-purpose flour
- 1 teaspoon salt
- 1 teaspoon black pepper
- 1 teaspoon paprika
- 1/2 teaspoon garlic powder
- Vegetable oil for frying

For the Waffles:

- 2 cups all-purpose flour
- 2 tablespoons sugar
- 1 tablespoon baking powder
- 1/2 teaspoon salt
- 2 large eggs
- 1 3/4 cups milk
- 1/2 cup unsalted butter, melted
- 1 teaspoon vanilla extract

For Assembly:

- Maple syrup
- Lettuce leaves
- Tomato slices
- Mayonnaise (optional)

Instructions:

Chicken:

In a bowl, marinate the chicken breasts in buttermilk for at least 30 minutes.
In a separate bowl, mix flour, salt, pepper, paprika, and garlic powder.
Heat vegetable oil in a skillet over medium-high heat.
Dredge each chicken breast in the flour mixture, ensuring an even coating.
Fry the chicken breasts until golden brown and cooked through, about 5-7 minutes per side.
Place on a paper towel to drain excess oil.

Waffles:

Preheat your waffle maker.
In a large bowl, whisk together flour, sugar, baking powder, and salt.
In another bowl, beat eggs and add milk, melted butter, and vanilla extract. Mix well.
Pour the wet ingredients into the dry ingredients and stir until just combined.
Cook waffles according to your waffle maker's instructions.

Assembly:

Place a fried chicken breast on a waffle.
Top with lettuce, tomato slices, and mayonnaise if desired.
Drizzle with maple syrup.
Place another waffle on top to create a sandwich.
Secure with toothpicks if needed.
Serve warm and enjoy the sweet and savory goodness!

Note:

- Customize with your favorite condiments or add a spicy kick with hot sauce.
- This recipe combines the classic flavors of fried chicken and waffles in a handheld sandwich for a delightful twist on a Southern favorite.

Mediterranean Chicken Pita

Ingredients:

For the Chicken:

- 1 pound boneless, skinless chicken breasts, thinly sliced
- 2 tablespoons olive oil
- 2 cloves garlic, minced
- 1 teaspoon dried oregano
- 1 teaspoon dried thyme
- Salt and pepper to taste
- Juice of 1 lemon

For the Tzatziki Sauce:

- 1 cup Greek yogurt
- 1 cucumber, finely diced
- 2 cloves garlic, minced
- 1 tablespoon fresh dill, chopped
- Salt and pepper to taste

For Assembly:

- Pita bread
- Cherry tomatoes, halved
- Red onion, thinly sliced
- Cucumber, thinly sliced
- Kalamata olives, pitted and sliced
- Feta cheese, crumbled
- Fresh parsley, chopped (for garnish)

Instructions:

Chicken:

In a bowl, combine olive oil, minced garlic, dried oregano, dried thyme, salt, pepper, and lemon juice.
Add sliced chicken to the marinade and coat evenly. Allow it to marinate for at least 30 minutes.

Heat a skillet over medium-high heat. Cook the marinated chicken slices until fully cooked and slightly browned. Set aside.

Tzatziki Sauce:

In a bowl, combine Greek yogurt, diced cucumber, minced garlic, chopped fresh dill, salt, and pepper.
Mix well until the ingredients are fully incorporated. Refrigerate until ready to use.

Assembly:

Warm the pita bread.
Spread a generous amount of tzatziki sauce on the inside of the pita.
Fill the pita with cooked Mediterranean chicken slices.
Add cherry tomatoes, red onion, cucumber, Kalamata olives, and crumbled feta.
Garnish with fresh parsley.
Serve immediately and enjoy the flavors of the Mediterranean in a delicious chicken pita!

Note:

- Customize with your favorite vegetables or add a drizzle of olive oil for extra richness.
- This recipe captures the essence of Mediterranean cuisine, combining seasoned chicken with vibrant veggies and the creamy goodness of tzatziki sauce in a satisfying pita sandwich.

Caprese Grilled Cheese

Ingredients:

- 4 slices of artisan bread
- 1 large ripe tomato, thinly sliced
- 8 fresh mozzarella slices
- Fresh basil leaves
- 2 tablespoons balsamic glaze
- 2 tablespoons unsalted butter
- Salt and pepper to taste

Instructions:

Lay out the slices of bread on a clean surface.
On two slices, layer fresh mozzarella, tomato slices, and fresh basil leaves.
Drizzle balsamic glaze over the tomato and basil layer.
Sprinkle a pinch of salt and pepper to taste.
Top each sandwich with the remaining slices of bread to create a sandwich.
Heat a non-stick skillet or griddle over medium heat.
Spread a thin layer of butter on the outside of each sandwich.
Place the sandwiches on the heated skillet and cook until the bread turns golden brown, and the cheese begins to melt (approximately 3-4 minutes per side).
Once both sides are golden brown and the cheese is melted, remove the sandwiches from the skillet.
Let them cool for a minute, then slice and serve immediately.

Note:

- The Caprese Grilled Cheese is a delightful twist on the classic sandwich, featuring the iconic combination of tomatoes, mozzarella, and basil. The addition of balsamic glaze elevates the flavors, creating a perfect harmony of tastes in every bite.

Smoked Turkey and Cranberry Wrap

Ingredients:

- 1 large whole wheat tortilla
- 6 slices of smoked turkey
- 2 tablespoons cream cheese
- 2 tablespoons cranberry sauce
- Handful of fresh spinach leaves
- 1/4 cup shredded cheddar cheese
- Salt and pepper to taste

Instructions:

Lay the whole wheat tortilla on a clean surface.
Spread a layer of cream cheese evenly over the tortilla.
Place the smoked turkey slices on top of the cream cheese.
Spoon cranberry sauce over the turkey.
Sprinkle shredded cheddar cheese over the cranberry sauce.
Add fresh spinach leaves on top of the cheese.
Season with salt and pepper to taste.
Carefully fold the sides of the tortilla inward and then roll it up tightly from the bottom to form a wrap.
Optional: Secure the wrap with toothpicks or wrap it in parchment paper for easier handling.
Slice the wrap in half diagonally and serve.

Note:

- The Smoked Turkey and Cranberry Wrap is a delightful combination of smoky turkey, creamy cream cheese, sweet cranberry sauce, and crunchy fresh spinach. It's a perfect blend of flavors and textures, making it a delicious and satisfying lunch option.

Spicy Tofu Banh Mi (Vegan)

Ingredients:

For Spicy Tofu:

- 1 block firm tofu, pressed and sliced into thin strips
- 2 tablespoons soy sauce
- 1 tablespoon sriracha sauce
- 1 tablespoon maple syrup
- 1 tablespoon rice vinegar
- 1 tablespoon sesame oil
- 1 teaspoon garlic powder
- 1 teaspoon onion powder
- 1 teaspoon smoked paprika
- 1 tablespoon vegetable oil for cooking

For Banh Mi:

- Baguette or Vietnamese-style bread
- Vegan mayonnaise
- Pickled daikon and carrots (store-bought or homemade)
- Cucumber, thinly sliced
- Fresh cilantro leaves
- Jalapeño, thinly sliced
- Hoisin sauce (optional)

Instructions:

For Spicy Tofu:

In a bowl, whisk together soy sauce, sriracha sauce, maple syrup, rice vinegar, sesame oil, garlic powder, onion powder, and smoked paprika to create a marinade.
Place sliced tofu in a shallow dish and pour the marinade over the tofu. Allow it to marinate for at least 30 minutes.
Heat vegetable oil in a pan over medium heat. Add marinated tofu slices and cook until golden brown on both sides.

For Banh Mi:

Slice the baguette or Vietnamese-style bread horizontally.
Spread a layer of vegan mayonnaise on both halves of the bread.
Arrange the cooked spicy tofu on the bottom half of the bread.
Layer with pickled daikon and carrots, cucumber slices, fresh cilantro leaves, and sliced jalapeños.
Drizzle hoisin sauce over the toppings if desired.
Place the top half of the bread over the fillings, press gently, and slice the sandwich into portions.
Serve the Spicy Tofu Banh Mi immediately and enjoy!

Note:

- This Spicy Tofu Banh Mi is a vegan twist on the classic Vietnamese sandwich. The combination of flavorful spicy tofu, crunchy pickled vegetables, and fresh herbs creates a delicious and satisfying meal.

Southwestern Black Bean Burger (Vegetarian)

Ingredients:

For Black Bean Patties:

- 2 cans (15 oz each) black beans, drained and rinsed
- 1 cup breadcrumbs
- 1/2 cup finely chopped red onion
- 1/2 cup corn kernels (fresh or frozen)
- 1/2 cup diced bell peppers (any color)
- 2 cloves garlic, minced
- 1 teaspoon ground cumin
- 1 teaspoon chili powder
- 1/2 teaspoon smoked paprika
- Salt and pepper to taste
- 2 tablespoons olive oil for cooking

For Chipotle Mayo:

- 1/2 cup mayonnaise
- 1 tablespoon adobo sauce from canned chipotle peppers
- 1 teaspoon lime juice

For Serving:

- Burger buns
- Lettuce leaves
- Sliced tomatoes
- Avocado slices
- Red onion rings

Instructions:

For Black Bean Patties:

In a large bowl, mash half of the black beans with a fork or potato masher. Leave the other half of the beans whole for texture.

Add breadcrumbs, red onion, corn, bell peppers, minced garlic, cumin, chili powder, smoked paprika, salt, and pepper to the mashed beans. Mix until well combined.

Form the mixture into burger patties.

Heat olive oil in a skillet over medium heat. Cook the black bean patties for about 4-5 minutes on each side or until they develop a golden-brown crust.

For Chipotle Mayo:

In a small bowl, mix together mayonnaise, adobo sauce, and lime juice until well combined.

For Serving:

Toast the burger buns.

Spread a generous amount of chipotle mayo on the bottom half of the bun.

Place a black bean patty on top of the mayo.

Layer with lettuce leaves, sliced tomatoes, avocado slices, and red onion rings.

Top with the other half of the bun.

Serve the Southwestern Black Bean Burger with your favorite side dishes and enjoy!

Note:

- This Southwestern Black Bean Burger offers a delicious blend of flavors and textures. The smoky and spicy chipotle mayo complements the hearty black bean patty, creating a satisfying vegetarian burger option.

BBQ Jackfruit Sandwich (Vegan)

Ingredients:

For BBQ Jackfruit:

- 2 cans (20 oz each) young green jackfruit in water or brine, drained and shredded
- 1 cup barbecue sauce
- 1 tablespoon olive oil
- 1 teaspoon smoked paprika
- 1 teaspoon garlic powder
- 1/2 teaspoon onion powder
- Salt and pepper to taste

For Coleslaw:

- 2 cups shredded cabbage (green or purple)
- 1 carrot, grated
- 1/2 cup vegan mayonnaise
- 1 tablespoon apple cider vinegar
- 1 tablespoon maple syrup
- Salt and pepper to taste

For Serving:

- Burger buns
- Pickles (optional)

Instructions:

For BBQ Jackfruit:

Heat olive oil in a skillet over medium heat. Add shredded jackfruit and sauté for 2-3 minutes.
Add smoked paprika, garlic powder, onion powder, salt, and pepper. Mix well.
Pour in the barbecue sauce and stir to coat the jackfruit evenly. Simmer for 15-20 minutes or until the jackfruit is tender and has absorbed the flavors.

For Coleslaw:

In a large bowl, combine shredded cabbage and grated carrot.

In a separate small bowl, whisk together vegan mayonnaise, apple cider vinegar, maple syrup, salt, and pepper.

Pour the dressing over the cabbage mixture and toss until well coated.

For Serving:

Toast the burger buns.

Spoon a generous amount of BBQ jackfruit onto the bottom half of the bun.

Top with a layer of coleslaw.

Add pickles if desired.

Place the other half of the bun on top.

Serve the BBQ Jackfruit Sandwich with additional coleslaw on the side and enjoy this vegan twist on a classic barbecue sandwich!

Note:

- BBQ jackfruit provides a satisfying and flavorful alternative to pulled pork. The combination of the smoky jackfruit and creamy coleslaw creates a delicious and cruelty-free sandwich option.

Turkey Reuben Wrap

Ingredients:

For Turkey Reuben Filling:

- 1 pound turkey breast, thinly sliced
- 1 cup sauerkraut, drained
- 8 slices Swiss cheese
- 1/2 cup Russian dressing
- 4 large whole-grain or rye tortillas

For Russian Dressing:

- 1/2 cup mayonnaise
- 2 tablespoons ketchup
- 1 tablespoon sweet pickle relish
- 1 teaspoon Worcestershire sauce
- Salt and pepper to taste

Instructions:

For Russian Dressing:

In a small bowl, whisk together mayonnaise, ketchup, sweet pickle relish, Worcestershire sauce, salt, and pepper.
Adjust the seasoning to taste. Set aside.

For Turkey Reuben Wrap:

Lay out each tortilla on a clean surface.
Spread a generous amount of Russian dressing on each tortilla, leaving a border around the edges.
Place a layer of turkey slices over the dressing on each tortilla.
Top the turkey with sauerkraut, dividing it evenly among the wraps.
Lay two slices of Swiss cheese over the sauerkraut on each tortilla.
Fold in the sides of the tortilla and then roll it up tightly to form a wrap.

Optional: Heat the wraps in a skillet or panini press for a warm and melty Reuben experience.
Slice the wraps in half diagonally.
Serve the Turkey Reuben Wraps with additional Russian dressing for dipping.
Enjoy this delicious twist on the classic Reuben sandwich with the goodness of turkey!

Note:

- This Turkey Reuben Wrap offers a lighter alternative to the traditional corned beef version while maintaining all the classic flavors. The Russian dressing adds a tangy kick to complement the savory turkey, sauerkraut, and Swiss cheese.

Portobello Mushroom and Goat Cheese Panini (Vegetarian)

Ingredients:

For the Portobello Mushrooms:

- 4 large portobello mushrooms, cleaned and sliced
- 2 tablespoons balsamic vinegar
- 2 tablespoons olive oil
- Salt and pepper to taste
- 1 teaspoon dried thyme

For the Panini:

- 8 slices of your favorite bread
- 1/2 cup goat cheese, crumbled
- 1 cup fresh spinach leaves
- 1 red onion, thinly sliced
- 2 tablespoons balsamic glaze (for drizzling)
- Butter or olive oil for grilling

Instructions:

For the Portobello Mushrooms:

In a bowl, mix balsamic vinegar, olive oil, salt, pepper, and dried thyme.
Place the portobello mushroom slices in the marinade, ensuring they are well coated. Let them marinate for at least 15 minutes.
Heat a grill pan or skillet over medium heat. Grill the portobello mushroom slices for about 3-4 minutes on each side, or until they are tender.
Remove from the heat and set aside.

For the Panini:

Preheat your panini press or grill pan.
Take each slice of bread and spread goat cheese on one side.
Place a layer of grilled portobello mushrooms on half of the bread slices.
Top the mushrooms with fresh spinach leaves and red onion slices.
Drizzle balsamic glaze over the vegetables.

Place the remaining slices of bread with goat cheese on top, forming sandwiches.
Lightly butter or brush olive oil on the outside of each sandwich.
Grill the sandwiches in the panini press or skillet until the bread is golden brown, and the goat cheese is melted.
Remove from the heat, slice, and serve hot.
Enjoy the delightful combination of earthy portobello mushrooms, tangy goat cheese, and vibrant veggies in this vegetarian panini!

Note:

- Feel free to customize the panini by adding other ingredients like roasted red peppers, arugula, or your favorite herbs.

California Veggie Wrap

Ingredients:

For the Avocado Spread:

- 1 ripe avocado, mashed
- 1 tablespoon lime juice
- Salt and pepper to taste

For the Wrap:

- 4 large whole wheat or spinach tortillas
- 1 cup hummus
- 1 cup cherry tomatoes, halved
- 1 cucumber, thinly sliced
- 1 cup shredded carrots
- 1 cup alfalfa sprouts or mixed microgreens
- 1/2 red onion, thinly sliced
- 1 cup baby spinach or arugula leaves
- Optional: Feta or goat cheese crumbles

Instructions:

For the Avocado Spread:

In a bowl, mash the ripe avocado.
Add lime juice, salt, and pepper to taste. Mix until well combined.

For the Wrap:

Lay out each tortilla on a flat surface.
Spread a generous layer of hummus onto each tortilla, leaving about an inch from the edges.
Evenly distribute the mashed avocado over the hummus layer.
Arrange cherry tomatoes, cucumber slices, shredded carrots, sprouts or microgreens, red onion slices, and baby spinach or arugula on top of the avocado.
If desired, sprinkle feta or goat cheese crumbles over the veggies.

Carefully fold in the sides of each tortilla, then roll it up tightly from the bottom to create a wrap.

Slice the wraps in half diagonally for serving.

Serve immediately and savor the fresh and vibrant flavors of this California-inspired veggie wrap.

Note:

Feel free to customize the wrap by adding grilled tofu, chickpeas, or your favorite protein for an extra boost of protein.

Pastrami on Rye

Ingredients:

- 8 slices of rye bread
- 1 pound of thinly sliced pastrami
- 1/2 cup Dijon mustard
- 1/2 cup mayonnaise
- 8 slices Swiss cheese
- 1 cup sauerkraut, drained
- 4 tablespoons unsalted butter, softened

Instructions:

Prepare the Spread:
- In a small bowl, mix Dijon mustard and mayonnaise until well combined.

Assemble the Sandwiches:
- Lay out 8 slices of rye bread.
- On each slice, spread a generous amount of the Dijon-mayo mixture.

Layer the Ingredients:
- On 4 slices of bread, layer the pastrami evenly.
- Top the pastrami with Swiss cheese slices.

Add Sauerkraut:
- Divide the sauerkraut equally among the 4 sandwiches, placing it on top of the Swiss cheese.

Complete the Sandwich:
- Place the remaining slices of bread (with the Dijon-mayo spread facing down) on top of the sauerkraut to complete the sandwiches.

Butter and Grill:
- Spread a thin layer of softened butter on the outer sides of each sandwich.

Grill the Sandwiches:
- In a skillet or pan over medium heat, grill each sandwich until the bread is toasted, and the cheese is melted. This usually takes 3-4 minutes per side.

Serve Warm:
- Once the sandwiches are golden brown and the cheese is gooey, remove them from the heat.
- Slice each sandwich diagonally and serve warm.

Note:

Feel free to adjust the amount of mustard and mayo in the spread to suit your taste preferences. You can also add pickles or additional condiments for extra flavor.

Moroccan Lamb Pita

Ingredients:

- 1 pound ground lamb
- 1 tablespoon olive oil
- 1 onion, finely chopped
- 2 cloves garlic, minced
- 1 teaspoon ground cumin
- 1 teaspoon ground coriander
- 1/2 teaspoon ground cinnamon
- 1/2 teaspoon paprika
- Salt and pepper to taste
- 1 cup Greek yogurt
- 2 tablespoons fresh mint, chopped
- 4 whole wheat pita bread
- Fresh vegetables for topping (tomatoes, cucumbers, lettuce, etc.)

Instructions:

Cook the Lamb:
- In a large skillet, heat olive oil over medium heat. Add chopped onions and garlic, sauté until softened.
- Add ground lamb to the skillet, breaking it apart with a spoon. Cook until browned.

Season the Lamb:
- Sprinkle cumin, coriander, cinnamon, paprika, salt, and pepper over the lamb. Mix well to combine. Allow the lamb to cook with the spices for an additional 5-7 minutes.

Prepare Yogurt Sauce:
- In a small bowl, mix Greek yogurt with chopped fresh mint. Set aside.

Warm the Pita:
- Toast the whole wheat pita bread in a toaster or warm them in the oven.

Assemble the Pitas:
- Spoon a generous portion of the spiced lamb mixture onto each warm pita.
- Top with a dollop of minty yogurt sauce.

Add Fresh Vegetables:

- Garnish with fresh vegetables of your choice. Sliced tomatoes, cucumbers, and lettuce work well.

Serve:
- Serve the Moroccan Lamb Pitas immediately while warm.

Note:

Feel free to customize the toppings based on your preferences. Consider adding olives, feta cheese, or a drizzle of tahini for extra flavor.

Turkey Avocado Ranch Wrap

Ingredients:

- 1 large whole wheat or spinach tortilla
- 6 ounces sliced turkey breast
- 1 ripe avocado, sliced
- 1/2 cup cherry tomatoes, halved
- 1/4 cup red onion, thinly sliced
- 1/2 cup mixed greens (lettuce or spinach)
- 2 tablespoons ranch dressing
- Salt and pepper to taste

Instructions:

Prepare Ingredients:
- Lay out the whole wheat or spinach tortilla on a clean surface.

Layer Turkey:
- Arrange the sliced turkey breast evenly over the tortilla.

Add Avocado:
- Place the sliced avocado over the turkey.

Sprinkle Tomatoes and Onion:
- Sprinkle halved cherry tomatoes and thinly sliced red onion on top.

Add Greens:
- Place a handful of mixed greens (lettuce or spinach) evenly across the wrap.

Drizzle with Ranch Dressing:
- Drizzle ranch dressing over the ingredients. Adjust the amount to your liking.

Season and Roll:
- Sprinkle a pinch of salt and pepper over the ingredients.
- Carefully fold in the sides of the tortilla and then roll it tightly from the bottom to create the wrap.

Slice and Serve:
- Use a sharp knife to slice the wrap in half diagonally.
- Serve immediately, or wrap it in parchment paper for an on-the-go lunch.

Note:

Feel free to customize the wrap with additional ingredients such as crispy bacon, shredded cheese, or your favorite hot sauce for an extra kick.

www.ingramcontent.com/pod-product-compliance
Lightning Source LLC
LaVergne TN
LVHW081611060526
838201LV00054B/2206